YOUR TEETH

WRITTEN BY ANNA STEARN

Celebration Press

Parsippany, New Jersey

Everybody needs strong, healthy teeth.

Teeth work with your tongue
to help you talk.

Teeth grind up your food to help you eat. They are the hardest parts of our bodies.

Kids have 20 baby teeth.
They will lose all 20. Then they
will grow 32 big teeth.

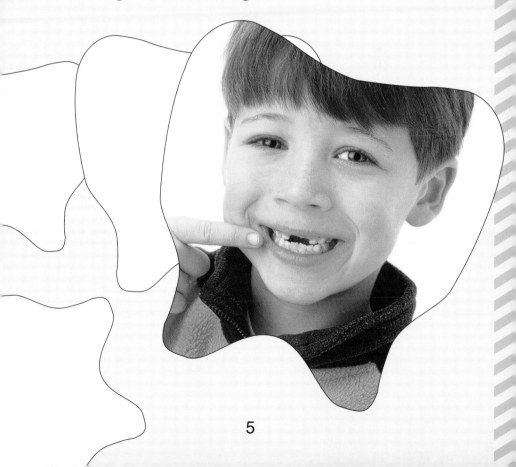

Some teeth have sharp edges. They are for biting food.

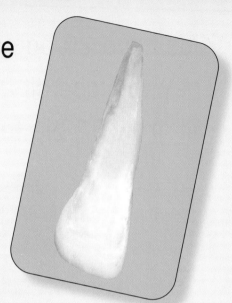

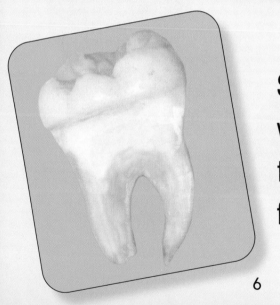

Some teeth have wide, bumpy tops. They are for grinding food.

Incisors and canines are for biting.
Molars are for grinding.

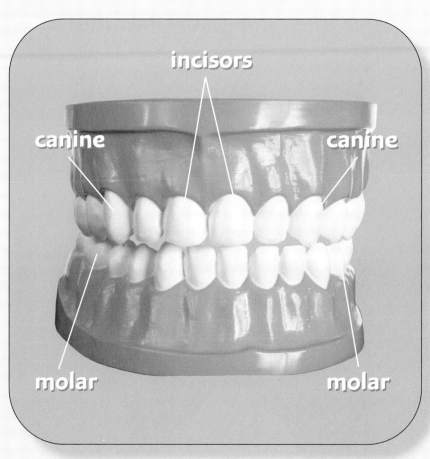

incisors

canine

canine

molar

molar

Brush and floss every day.
Take care of your teeth
and they will last a lifetime!